The Raising of Money

Thirty-Five Essentials
Every Trustee Should Know

James Gregory Lord

THIRD SECTOR PRESS
Cleveland

Fourteenth Printing, July, 1989

Published by
Third Sector Press
2000 Euclid Avenue
P.O. Box 18044
Cleveland, Ohio 44118
216/831-9300

Copyright © MCMLXXXIII
by James Gregory Lord

All rights reserved. No part of this book may be reproduced
in any form or by any electronic or mechanical means, including information storage and retrieval systems or photocopy, without permission in writing from the publisher,
except by a reviewer who may quote brief passages in a
review.

Library of Congress Cataloging in Publication Data

Lord, James Gregory
    The Raising of Money.
    Includes index, bibliography

    ISBN 0-939120-02-X   LC: 84-50377

    Manufactured in the United States of America

**Multiple copies of this book are available from the publisher
at substantial discounts.**

Spanish and French editions available soon.

Dedication

To the Volunteer

The volunteer, the advocate, is the heart and soul of philanthropy.

Working my way across the country as a consultant, I would often arrive in a community that was new to me. One thought always emerged: I would soon be meeting "the best people when they're at their best."

They would be the best—because they would be the most successful and respected, by any measure our society uses. And they would be at their best—because they would be giving of their energies and resources in a voluntary spirit.

The result of their commitment would be to enrich the quality of people's lives—and, in fact, to advance our civilization.

There is no greater honor than to serve these people, these advocates. They are, indeed, "the best at their best."

The Third Sector

One of the great strengths of free societies is the availability of *choice*. Nowhere is this principle demonstrated so clearly as in our philanthropic organizations—where people freely choose to devote their own time, talents and resources to enhancing the quality of our lives.

In the twentieth century, these institutions—commonly called the "non-profits"—have become so important to our way of life that they have been renamed the *Third Sector* of our society.

Any society needs healthy business and government sectors. We have now come to realize that in order to *advance our civilization,* we need a healthy Third Sector. That is its very reason for being.

Acknowledgments

The greatest inspiration for this book was provided by the volunteers and the donors with whom I have been privileged to work—people like Joseph B. Dahlkemper of Erie, Pennsylvania.

Once, when I asked him why he thought philanthropy was important, Mr. Dahlkemper paused for a moment, looked into the distance and began to speak from the heart:

> My grandparents were farmers. When I was a child, I asked them why they sometimes turned crops back into the soil, instead of harvesting them. They told me that the earth had been good to them, and if they wanted it to continue to be productive, they needed to return something to the ground.
>
> Isn't that what we're doing in our community? Isn't that why philanthropy makes so much sense?

Behind these volunteers are the professionals who manage development programs. So many have taught me so much.

Among the others to whom a debt is owed:

- Harold J. "Si" Seymour—who made a lasting contribution to the literature of the field with his still-quoted *Designs for Fund Raising* and other occasional papers, which provided me with much inspiration.
- My wife, Wendy—who gave the sustenance that allowed the inspiration to be committed to paper.
- Derek VanPelt—who, as my editor, helped me understand what I was trying to say; and as this book's designer, made it look good. His friendship, and his knowledge of fund raising and marketing, have been most valuable.
- R. Blair Schreyer, president of Ketchum, Inc. and past chairman of the American Association of Fund-Raising Counsel—who delivered me into the world of capital campaigns more than a dozen years ago.
- . . . And the Ben Kaufmans of this world.

To all these; to the many others who have invested their time in reading the manuscript and providing advice and ideas; and to the hundreds who have labored through this material with me as I tested it in speeches, seminars and workshops—I say, "Thank you for the benefit of your talents."

Introduction

This is a book about *people*—how they feel, how they think and act, and what happens between them when they're engaged in the enterprise of philanthropy.

The intent of this small volume is to report what we've come to understand about this phenomenon. On these pages can be found the most important principles of fund raising—no more, and no less. At least, that is our intention.

We have not attempted to cover every facet of philanthropy, every fund-raising technique. The focus is on the art and science of campaigning and face-to-face solicitation. The reasons should become apparent.

This book reflects an increasingly specific approach to the raising of funds. It's an approach that asks us to be more intentional, more organized and more strategic than we used to be. The focus is less on getting donations *per se,* and more on the development of donors and the development of institutions.

This is not a "how-to" manual on fund raising. In the day-to-day practice of philanthropy, most decisions are "judgment calls" that depend on circumstance and opportunity. This book will serve only as a backdrop against which this drama is played out.

In the final analysis, raising money is a *personal* business. Results will come from people, not from books. As Shakespeare said, "Action is eloquence."

Preface

On Brevity

In 1656, Pascal wrote to a friend: "I have only made this letter rather long because I have not had time to make it short."

That's still the way it is. It takes *more* time to make a communication short and to the point than it does to spill forth all our thoughts and ideas.

People resent the time they have to spend reading or listening for information. Most don't really read much at all; they skim.

When we communicate with people, as much thought needs to go into what *shouldn't* be said as what should be said.

In making a case to a prospective donor, for example, many organizations try to give the prospect every possible reason to contribute. This accomplishes two things:

1. It demonstrates a lack of confidence and clarity on the part of the organization.

2. It's *boring*. "The man with the unimpressive argument," as the saying goes, "rattles off many of them."

The only person who's really interested in reading or listening to a long-winded monologue is the person who writes or delivers it.

So in writing this book, we've tried to take the time to make it short.

We hope that when you lay it down, you'll feel that the words of Winston Churchill might, in some measure, apply:

"Out of intense complexities, intense simplicities emerge."

Other works by James Gregory Lord:

Philanthropy and Marketing:
  Strategies for Fund-Raising
Building Your Case: Seminar and Workshop in a Box
Results! Time Management System
Foreword to *The Best of Marketing from Harvard Busi-*
  ness Review
Foreword to *The Perfect Development Officer*
Spanish Translation of *The Raising of Money*
                                    — *and others*

Also available from Third Sector Press

The Campaign Manuals: Forms, Plans, Samples and
  Checklists
The Campaign Letter
The Non-Profit Management Reports
The Development Consultant
Non-Profit Management Forms: Charts, Formats,
  Graphs and Worksheets to Photocopy
Think Sheets
How to Work Smarter, Not Harder: A Management
  Manual for Development Officer by John William
  Zehring
Fund Raising Letters by Jerry Huntsinger
                                    — and others

TABLE OF CONTENTS

Dedication i
The Third Sector iii
Acknowledgments v
Introduction vii
Preface: On Brevity ix

I

Working from the Perspective of the Marketplace

Organizations Have No Needs 3
Seek Investment, Not Charity 4
Position Your Organization Relative
   to Its Competition 7
Listen to the Donor Community 11
Listen to What Each Donor Has to Say 12
Donors Will Tell You What They Want 15
Make Your Case Larger Than the Institution ... 18

II

Getting People Involved

Go for the Gold 25
Create Authentic Involvement 29
The Process of Planning Is More Important
    Than the Plan Itself 32
Share Your Plans Without Asking for Money .. 36
Use a Feasibility Study to Build a Strategy 39

III

Setting the Pace for Giving

If You Seek Average Gifts,
    You Get Below-Average Results 45
A Few Will Do the Most 47
The Early Donor Sets the Pace 49
Trustees Have an Opportunity,
    Not an Obligation 52
Staff Giving Lends Credibility 54
Make Great Investments Possible 56

IV

Applying the Campaign Principle

People Prefer Structure 61
Take One Step at a Time 63

Scheduling Creates Momentum 65
Build a Sense of Campaign 67
Create a Climate of Universality 68
Winning Is Fundamental 69
Meetings Keep Things Moving 70

V

Asking for Money

People Give to People 75
The Right Person Makes the Difference 78
The One Who Asks Must First Give 79
See Each Prospect Face to Face 80
Ask for a Specific Amount; Ask for Enough ... 81
Qualify the Prospect 83
Tenacity Prevails 86
Ask for the Order 87

VI

Practicing Stewardship

The Donor Deserves Good Stewardship 91

VII

Kindling the Spirit of Philanthropy

The Best Advocate Is Both Donor
    and Volunteer 97

A Word on Fund-Raising Professionals and Consultants

Hire The Best—and Let Them Direct 101
Counsel Can Help to Ensure Success 105

Quotations

Philanthropy 111
Voluntarism 113
Goals and Accomplishments 115

About the Author 119
Suggested Reading 121
Index 125

The Raising
of Money

I

Working from the Perspective of the Marketplace

The days of hand-wringing and arm-twisting are drawing to a close. Today, the successful organization invites people to invest in a worthy enterprise.

Organizations Have No Needs

Trying to raise money on the basis of an organization's needs will work just about as well as trying to obtain a bank loan by pleading poverty. Panhandling is as ineffective with donors as it is with bankers.

Too many institutions still haven't accepted this reality. They continue to believe that the more desperate for funds they appear, the more successful at fund raising they'll be.

But donors are tired of hearing these pleas over and over again. In fact, from the viewpoint of the donor, an organization *has no needs*.

A community, of course, may have needs to satisfy. Society may have problems to solve. People may have needs and problems.

The organization has solutions. It has answers. It has capabilities.

Successful organizations today are putting philanthropic dollars to work in meeting the needs of *people*.

Those who really have an edge on the competition go a step further, beyond the community's needs and society's problems.

These organizations address people's *wants*. They address the community's potential and society's aspirations. They address *opportunities*—and show how the institution is poised to capitalize on these opportunities, on behalf of all those it serves.

One urban university translated this attitude into words when it described itself as "an instrument for the advancement of society."

Other institutions, unfortunately, still behave as if their own internal agendas are more important than their mission of service to society. What Napoleon said about human nature more than 150 years ago can still be applied to them:

"Men take only their needs into consideration, never their abilities."

Seek Investment, Not Charity

Invite your prospective donor to make a wise investment that will produce benefits. Donors are tired of giving handouts to the needy.

John D. Rockefeller, Jr. said it well: "Never think you need to apologize for asking someone to give to a worthy object, any more than as though you were giving him an opportunity to participate in a high-grade investment."

For some reason, those of us involved in philanthropy used to think we were in the generosity business.

We operated on the premise that our organizations were entitled to charity—like the beggar who stationed himself every day near the office of a wealthy businessman. The beggar had received a dime a day from the businessman over a long period of time.

The businessman went out of town for a month. When he returned, he passed the beggar, who said to him with a slight tone of reproach, "You owe me three dollars."

Institutions are not entitled to charity. The days of hand-wringing and arm-twisting are drawing to a close.

Institutions must earn and attract *investment*. The ones that are advancing today are the ones in which people choose to invest.

The fact is that people give in order to *get*. They don't want to feel that they are "giving away" their money. They want to feel that they are investing it, and getting something in return.

The Boys Clubs of America, for example, works with young people to build self-respect and self-reliance, and to combat crime and delinquency. Its theme is: "If we can help them now, then they can help us later."

The organization invites donors to invest in solid, productive citizens. It doesn't ask them to fund a deficit.

In the raising of funds—as in the providing of services—the key words are *achievement, accomplishment, performance* and *success*.

One of the nation's leading resident theatres used to appeal for funds on the basis of its own internal needs. The theatre felt it could count on the traditional generosity of the city's theatre lovers to "keep the doors open."

Then the institution realized that if it was ever going to expand its constituency beyond this family of insiders, it would have to present itself differently. The theatre began to look at the priorities of community leaders and to consider which ones the institution was in a position to help achieve.

Leading individuals and businesses in the city were concerned with building civic pride and improving the city's image nationally and internationally. As it happened, the theatre's facilities were located in the central city, and had been for more than 80 years. And not only did the theatre enjoy an international reputation; its name also incorporated the name of the city.

Therefore, a new fund-raising strategy was adopted. For the first time in years, the theatre didn't plead for help in order to avoid a deficit. Instead, it presented itself as a community asset that carried the city's name worldwide. The theatre portrayed itself as an enterprise in which those who cared about the city could invest.

The new strategy was successful. One of the results was that the theatre was able to complete its season without conducting its usual "spring beg" (as the volunteers used to call it). Another was that leading citizens who had never been theatre lovers became enthusiastic donors and volunteers.

This theatre adopted the marketplace perspective. It realized that the center of its universe is not the institution, but the *marketplace*—the donor community. It realized that the interests and aspirations of the *donor* come first.

This transition from begging to marketing is one of the most profound changes in philanthropy in recent years. Unfortunately, this new reality has yet to dawn on most institutions, which continue to maintain an inwardly focused and myopic point of view.

We don't have to be greedy. Money, it's said, flows in a stream. Having to "go to the well," as if there's only so much, is a mistaken notion. There's really quite enough money to be had—if only we show how the money will be wisely invested.

Position Your Organization Relative to Its Competition

The most attractive organizations stand out from the crowd. They're the ones that know how to distinguish themselves as investment opportunities.

The attractive organization has adopted a stance that sets it apart from others which compete for the attention of donors and volunteers.

How is this done? Using a method developed by business, the organization *positions* itself in the philanthropic marketplace. The key is to answer two questions:

1. What does the organization do well—or what *can* it do well—that matters to its prospects?
2. How does that compare to what other organizations have to offer?

A museum, for example, does not compete only with other museums. In the eyes of the prospect, it also competes with colleges, performing arts groups, and even hospitals and social service agencies.

The competition is even broader than that. The museum, and every other organization, also tends to compete with the family, religion and work—the things that most folks put first.

So in positioning an organization, we need to understand what's on our prospect's mind—and to align our program with his or her established interests and priorities.

We need to think marketing, not selling. If we're offering something the prospect *already wants,* the "sale" comes naturally.

It's said, for example, that Black & Decker manufactures drills, but its customers buy holes. Charles Revson, founder of Revlon, said, "In the factory, we make cosmetics. In the stores, we sell hope."

How people see an institution, and even what they call it, depends on where they're standing. In much of

8

the world, observed Al Ries and Jack Trout in their book *Positioning,* "The People's Republic of China is usually called Red China because no one believes it is a *people's* republic. (Inside the country, the People's Republic of China is undoubtedly an effective name)."

Closer to home, the Metropolitan Opera is widely considered not only the nation's best opera company, but the only one that tours enough to be considered a true national resource. That's the position it owns in many people's minds.

Another example: One major research university, located in a northern industrial state, was preparing for a capital campaign. At the same time, the state's leadership was trying to encourage high-technology industries and diversify the economy.

The university emphasized that it could help the state accomplish this goal by joining with business in research and development ventures.

This institution had identified its *distinctive competency*—the major benefit it was in a position to provide better than anyone else. An investment in the university would be an investment in high-tech prosperity.

A campaign slogan is often used to position the enterprise in the minds of its constituents. It serves as a constant reminder of the major benefit—what the campaign is all about.

One small and relatively unknown Midwestern college adopted as its campaign theme "The First Generation Campaign." This phrase emphasized the college's specialty: its expertise in educating first-generation college students.

This was a service that mattered to the leaders in the city where the college was located. It struck them as a worthwhile investment.

The college surprised many observers by attracting the city's top leadership to its campaign organization. The success of the campaign could be attributed, in no small measure, to shrewd positioning.

By aligning itself with the values and priorities of the leaders, this college distinguished itself from dozens of "good little colleges" who were seeking the support of the same people.

Many of these schools continue to struggle for survival—because they haven't succeeded in convincing anyone but their own faculty and alumni that they have a special role to play. Without a distinctive stance in the philanthropic marketplace, they face an uphill battle.

Listen to the Donor Community

"I've got to follow them; I am their leader."
—*Alexandre Ledru-Rollin*

If you want to help an organization to advance, the first step is really quite simple: Stop focusing on internal issues long enough to get outside the organization—and ask people what they think of it, and what they want from it.

It's essential to listen to the donor community. If we can find out what's on *their* minds and where *they're* going, we'll be in a strong position to shape our offering accordingly.

If we're not tuned in to what the donor community is saying, we can easily get in trouble—for we may end up trying to coerce people. We may find ourselves trying to convince people how they *should* think and what they *should* do.

It's much easier to relate our program to what people already want.

For example, the public televison and radio facility in a major Southern city recently had to raise a lot of money to upgrade its technical equipment. The organization realized that on its face, this was a drab and uninspiring proposition for the donor.

But this organization kept its ear to the ground. It knew that the city harbored a certain "inferiority complex" that its leaders badly wanted to overcome. So the station proposed to do something about it.

11

Better equipment, the station explained, would mean *better programs* about the city. Better programs would mean that people would *feel better* about their city. And if the programs were good enough, they might get national attention, helping to improve the city's image everywhere.

This organization listened to its constituents; and it shaped its offering to harmonize with their interests. As a result, the campaign exceeded its goal by a comfortable margin.

Any organization is more likely to succeed in raising funds if it's really listening to the donor community—to the groups that have the capacity to *bring about* success.

Listen to What Each Donor Has to Say

The "donor community" isn't an abstraction. It's made up of flesh-and-blood *people* with their own personal attitudes and preferences.

Some of these people can turn an organization's dreams into realities—but only if we listen to them as individuals, find out what they want, and make our approach accordingly.

After all, it's been proven that the success of any program will, in the end, be determined by a very few people. Each of these, as one seasoned campaign manager observes, "is a campaign unto itself."

If a prospective donor is interested in cancer research, for example, it makes little sense to try to convince that prospect that he or she *should* contribute to a pediatric wing (no matter how much the institution needs one).

Our time will be better spent in hearing the prospect. We want to give the prospect an opportunity to tell us his or her vision of what could be. Only then can we design an appropriate response.

"When I'm getting ready to reason with a man," said Abraham Lincoln, "I spend one-third of my time thinking about myself and what I am going to say, and two-thirds thinking about him and what he is going to say."

A little imagination and creativity can go a long way in "making the match" between prospect and program.

A major zoo was looking for a way to get a certain corporate leader interested in its program. Zoos had never been especially high on his list of priorities. He was an entrepreneur who was known for investing in education, and in projects that promoted free-enterprise values.

Realizing this, the institution didn't attempt to interest this individual in its capital construction program. Instead, the zoo proposed that he invest in its education department—which was distinguished by a special approach.

This zoo taught young people about human society by showing them how "animal societies" worked. The basic principles of competition, cooperation, adaptation and survival were related to the children's own future in a free society. This program provided the entrepreneur with an unusual opportunity to invest in the values that were most important to him.

Certainly, the interests of the donor community as a whole are important. So are the wants and needs of the institution's users—its students, clients, patrons or patients.

But when we want to win over a particular *individual*, what counts most is that person's own thoughts, concerns and aspirations. Rather than making the same case to everyone, we need to listen and respond on a *personal* level.

Benjamin Franklin, not surprisingly, had some choice advice for us: "If you would persuade, you must appeal to interest, rather than the intellect."

Donors Will Tell You
What They Want

How do you find out what's going on in a person's mind? Psychologist George Kelly suggested, "Ask him; he may tell you."

Kelly's observation, obvious though it may seem, tends to escape us all from time to time. As the development of institutions becomes a more sophisticated "science," we devote considerable energy and resources to prospect research. We compile data on donors from every available source, *except the donor.*

The donor is the best source of all. We sometimes forget that most people like to be sought out for their opinions. A single face-to-face interview can be worth more than volumes of research. And we can learn quite a lot by developing the habit of attentive listening in the course of our daily activities.

Besides casual conversation, what other ways are there to find out what people want?

We'll go into more detail later—but in the raising of money, there are at least three:

1. Use mail or telephone surveys (but only if you don't have the time or resources to see people personally).

2. Create opportunities for dialogue with community leaders about your institution and its plans. One avenue is the "leadership awareness program."

3. Conduct a series of confidential, one-on-one interviews with community leaders—a feasibility study.

The point is that simply putting the right questions to a few of the right people can generate a wealth of valuable insights.

Here's an example of what can happen through a structured listening process.

One major university was contemplating a huge capital campaign that incorporated a number of programs. The personal priority of the university president was a new art gallery. Most of the "insiders" felt that a new cancer hospital would be most attractive to donors.

To find out what would work, the university conducted a series of interviews with some of its key donors. Surprise! The art gallery and cancer hospital were well received—but most people felt that strengthening the *faculty* should be the highest priority.

What's more, the donors had their own ideas about which departments should be developed. The university had provided its own list of faculty chairs to be endowed. These met with a cool response.

This university understood that it wouldn't be a good idea to make its plans in a vacuum, or to guess what people *might* think of its ideas. This institution was sharp enough to ask—early enough so that its plans could be shaped accordingly.

Of course, there are values and other motivations that run deeper than current interests. Why *do* people give? It's a fascinating study.

In his book, *Designs for Fund-Raising,* Harold J. "Si" Seymour postulated that people aspire simply "to be sought." Seymour also cited a study by Dr. Dorothea Leighton, an anthropologist, who concluded that each of us needs to feel we are "a worthwhile member of a worthwhile group."

Many people who have been in this business for a long time feel that the key motivating factor is self-image. We all strive to bring our behavior into line with the way we think of ourselves. ("This is the kind of person I am.")

Understanding what people want is critical to the practice of fund raising. Not to ask them—to assume that we *already* know—is an oversight we can ill afford. It certainly is a human trait, though.

I'm reminded of an experience the reader has undoubtedly shared with me. You're in a restaurant, you've finished your meal, and you ask the waiter, "What can you offer for dessert?"

The waiter replies, "We only have apple pie today."

Little did he know that until that moment, at least, apple pie was exactly what you wanted. The poor fellow could see things only from his own viewpoint. He presumed to know what his "prospect" *didn't* want.

We never know what our prospect wants—until we ask.

Make Your Case
Larger Than the Institution

The effective case for support is like an investment prospectus for a business. It is designed to attract donors—who are, after all, investors.

But the case is also like a good speech or the closing remarks of an attorney. It is designed to move people both intellectually and emotionally.

The right facts and the logic must be there: what the organization has accomplished; what it has the potential to do; and what benefits the investment will bring. But the facts alone won't carry the day.

When a case is written for donors, it has to touch them where they live and breathe. They need to feel that investing in the program will make life better for them, for their children and grandchildren. They need to feel that the community and the nation will be strengthened—even that *civilization itself* will be advanced by what they do.

The best casemakers have found that in order to move people on this level, it's essential to make your case *larger than the institution*. It's not enough to "tell the story" of the organization, to recite its history. It's equally ineffective to try to convince the prospect that the organization needs the money to avoid deterioration or collapse.

What works best is to present a vision of the future—one that people find attractive, achievable and worth working for. The case demonstrates how the institution can make a special contribution to building that future. Prospects must be *inspired and challenged* to play a part in making it happen. They should feel that they have a chance to make history—and that the time for action is now.

The best cases can be summed up in a few powerful sentences, or even a single memorable phrase. This kind of case is easy for volunteers to internalize, and to articulate to their prospects. The case shouldn't attempt to "cover the waterfront" by including every conceivable reason to support the program.

To bring the vision into focus, the case must include the facts, the data and the dollars to support the argument. Certainly, people want to know how many National Merit scholars the school is producing. Donors are interested in your distinctive, innovative programs—your success stories. Give them examples, illustrations, case histories. But don't drown them in data. All the "vital statistics" belong somewhere else; the case itself should be simple and brief.

The effective case also gives evidence of the *planning* behind the program. It shows prospects that the organization is managed in a businesslike way. And it explains how their investments will be applied in a timely fashion to the areas where they will produce the best results, the greatest benefits.

This kind of case can't be developed from an internal, institutional perspective. It has to be psychologically based in the donor marketplace.

Experience has shown that the strongest arguments come from those who will give and work for the cause—from their deepest concerns, desires and aspirations. It makes sense to involve them in *developing* the case, not just approving it.

In other words, we should take our cues from the people who can make the program a success. They should be interviewed and even quoted in the case. When this is done, the case often turns out to be more useful *before* it's finished.

One Midwestern college, for example, was developing its case for an upcoming capital campaign. A certain trustee, a successful businessman, was interviewed for his input.

This philanthropist had previously endowed a center for free-enterprise education at the college. He chose this particular school because it openly advocated our nation's free social, political and economic institutions.

The resulting case positioned the institution as an unusual investment opportunity for those who wanted to advance the same values. The theme was "A Time of Opportunity."

The point was that it was a "time of opportunity" not only for the donor and for the college, but for the nation as well. President Reagan had just taken office, and the business community was extraordinarily optimistic about the future.

The trustee was quoted in the case. Partly because he had played an important role in building the case, and saw his own deepest aspirations reflected in the college's development program, he became an even more enthusiastic advocate. He was instrumental in bringing the campaign, the largest ever attempted by the school, to a highly successful conclusion.

Because this man was moved both intellectually and emotionally, he had developed a *sense of ownership* of the institution and its program. He acted with conviction because he felt that he was promoting his own best interests—and those of the college, the nation and civilization itself.

That's how much an effective case can accomplish. We shouldn't be satisfied with a list of needs or tired slogans about "continuing the traditions." The case that seeks out the prospect's responsive chord, and resonates with it, is the case that produces action.

II

Getting People Involved

*The way to raise real money
is to provide real involvement.
So put people before dollars.*

Go for the Gold

The best person to lead your program is the one who has a reputation for allowing nothing to fail.

This type of leader—the type whose presence creates confidence—is rare.

Most volunteers can be grouped into three other categories: the *responsible* (those we can rely on to follow through); the *responsive* (those we can hope to move); and the *unresponsive*. "Si" Seymour says of this last group: "The finest rhetoric never reaches these people, if only because they are not there to listen."

People have been trying for centuries, without success, to change a lump of lead into a nugget of gold. In enlisting volunteer leadership, it's best to begin by "going for the gold" —the winners. After that, perhaps, some alchemy can be used to develop the *next* generation of leaders.

"One of the best ways to predict the success or failure of any fund-raising program," says one veteran campaign director, "is to ask: 'Have people of stature been enlisted as active members of the campaign team?'"

First-class people doing a first-class job—that breeds achievement.

Influence flows downward, so begin at the top. It's easier to enlist the vice president, for example, if you've already enlisted the president—not the other way around.

What makes for good leadership? Most experienced fund-raisers look for these qualities:

1. *Affluence*—the ability to make a substantial contribution.

2. *Influence*—the ability to attract others to volunteer and to make substantial contributions.

3. *Availability*—the willingness to give priority attention to the program.

4. *Team spirit*—the willingness to provide voluntary leadership *and* to accept professional direction.

Some would add to this list "interest in the cause." While this is certainly helpful, it's secondary. If interest is already present, wonderful. If not, it can be developed.

Those who are already close to your cause are the obvious choices, and may be easier to enlist. If they meet the four criteria, you want them on your team. People will certainly expect the trustees, for example, to be active.

But by enlisting people who are identified with the *community*—not necessarily with the institution—you'll help to build a sense that it's the community's

26

campaign, not just a self-serving effort by the organization.

For example, when the board of a small Catholic hospital tapped a non-Catholic to lead its campaign, the response from the community was unusually enthusiastic.

"He's not on the board," people said. "He's not even Catholic." This enlistment succeeded in communicating to people that the project was important to the town, beyond the organization's provincial concerns.

When the campaign headquarters is placed in a bank building, rather than "on campus"; or when the campaign chairman uses his or her personal letterhead, rather than the institution's, the same message comes through.

The most successful organizations are those who make their campaign the *community's* campaign—and who pass the torch of leadership and ownership to those who can make things happen for the organization.

"Going for the gold," and getting it, isn't easy. First-class leaders are in short supply, busy and sought after. In a way, you're competing more for volunteers than for money.

"It's easy to get people to give," says Samuel Belzberg, Chairman of First City Financial in Vancouver. "What's tough is to get them to ask." When you put the giver and asker together in one person, then you have success.

In our quest to enlist such leaders, we need to be as thoughtful, strategic and persistent as we are in soliciting a six-figure contribution. (In fact, if we've thought it through, our candidates for the top leadership posts may well be our best financial prospects.)

One small college, for example, wanted to recruit one of the community's most successful businessmen to chair its campaign. A veteran of many campaigns, this executive was nearing retirement and thought to be uninterested in leading another effort.

The school's strategy was to first recruit several other corporate leaders for the campaign cabinet— people respected by the reluctant candidate. The college then surrounded him with those already enlisted. One by one, each indicated to him: "We can't do this without you. We want you to lead us."

The college also presented the executive with a short list of the chairman's responsibilities, including how many hours would be required each month. The candidate, a victim of disarray and overwork in past campaigns, found this reassuring.

After giving it some thought, the executive accepted the job. The campaign went over its goal, as one might expect.

In the enlistment of volunteer leadership, it's best not to take the line of least resistance. Go for the gold; you just might get it.

Create Authentic Involvement

Involvement, it is said, is more important than information. If we want people to invest their time and resources in a program, we have to give them *authentic* involvement in the cause.

"Pretend participation"—a name on a letterhead—isn't enough. Neither is a seat on a board that has no important function. True leaders easily see through these ploys.

We want people to feel involved with our causes the same way they are involved with their families, their work, their religion. The volunteer deserves to feel that the organization is a vital part of his or her everyday life.

The best way to develop that sense of involvement is to invite a person to *do something important* for us—something he or she is especially qualified and suited to do.

The donor will then begin to become an *insider.* Once that happens, he or she will have a greater stake in the success of the institution—and a greater willingness to contribute to that success.

Take, for example, a trustee of a certain university in a medium-sized industrial city. He had been on the board for a few years. A fine gentleman and president of a Fortune 500 company, he had no reason to do much more for the university than attend the semi-annual board meetings.

When a capital campaign was contemplated, it was clear that he should be interviewed in the feasibility study. His views would be important because of who he was in his own right. He also represented the type of people who would have to become part of this enterprise, if it were to achieve its goal.

The university benefitted from the interview—not only because of what it learned, but because the act of consulting this executive for his views increased his involvement.

Following the study, he was invited to serve on the development committee of the board. Through this role, he became even more of an insider. The members of this group were to review and approve the university's ten-year development plan, and each agreed to host a meeting of a small group of community leaders to discuss the plan.

Not long after joining this committee, the executive agreed to serve as general chairman of the campaign. He had become genuinely involved in the school.

This involvement increased as he assisted with setting the campaign goal, identifying prospects and evaluating their capacity to give. He also identified prospective volunteers, enlisted them and asked them to contribute.

As the general chairman, he often worked in a team with the university president and other key volunteers. The more people who joined in enlisting and soliciting, the more widely the case was made, and the more people had a stake in the success of the program.

A donor's involvement need not be limited to fund raising. In fact, when people take part in the general business of an institution, they become more committed to its success. One could argue that the donor should have as much to say about the future of the institution as the stockholder does about the future of the company. As investors, both are entitled to influence the setting of policy.

This principle of authentic involvement applies before, during and after raising funds. It is the best way to move someone (who deserves the role) from being an outsider to being an insider—and finally to enable that person to develop a *sense of ownership* of the organization.

This is a basic *quid pro quo* in the business of development. Too many organizations still try to get around it. If we want real dollars and real work from people, then we must provide them with real involvement. If we want token dollars and token work, then we can provide token involvement.

When we recruit investors, we must give them a share of ownership. It's a process of exchange; we owe them. As many a businessman is fond of saying, "There's no free lunch"—not from government, and not from philanthropy, either.

The Process of Planning Is More Important Than the Plan Itself

Without a strategy based on a knowledge of the philanthropic marketplace, there will be only random ideas without a guiding purpose. As the Roman philosopher Seneca said, "When a man does not know what harbor he is making for, no wind is the right wind."

Or, as Yogi Berra put it more recently, "You've got to be very careful if you don't know where you are going, because you might not get there."

So an organization has to have a plan for its future—particularly when it's preparing to embark on a fund-raising campaign or a long-range development program. If for no other reason, people deserve to know how you intend to use the money—and what kind of benefits are expected.

The beginning of a development program, especially a capital campaign, automatically attracts attention. Getting ready for the campaign provides a special opportunity to rethink priorities; recommit loyalties; and redirect energies.

What makes planning even more valuable is the opportunity it presents for good old *involvement*. "The primary benefit of the planning process is the process itself, and not a plan," writes George A. Steiner in *Strategic Planning*. If an organization's leaders are on the ball, they will use the planning process to get people involved in mapping the organization's future—

especially those people who have the power to help *bring about* that future.

Authentic involvement in the planning process can promote a sense of ownership among prospective donors and volunteers. People are simply more motivated to work for, and invest in, the realization of plans they themselves have helped to develop.

(There must, of course, be a time when the focus shifts from planning to implementation. Beware of "paralysis by analysis.")

The act of planning also focuses and clarifies the thinking. This is another way in which the process itself is more important than the resulting document.

Furthermore, in the development field, planning makes the organization look good. Most donors don't want to know all the details—but they *do* want to be assured that you "have your ducks in a row." They want to be shown that you're using the skills of the business world, and that you're treating your enterprise in an intentional, organized and strategic manner.

You'll make an excellent impression if you can tell people that your organization has:

• Conducted surveys among the people your organization serves;

• Designed a strategic or business plan for the organization; and

• Produced a financial plan for the next five years or more.

This kind of planning is exactly what one philanthropist wanted when he asked a hospital trustee:

"What's your mission? And I don't mean that formal stuff, either. What *are* you doing? What does your five-year plan look like? What services are you going to add? To abandon?"

More and more prospects are asking these tough questions. Too many organizations still have no answers, or only the vaguest ones. The sharp organizations, those that are attracting big money, are ready with their plans.

Corporations, foundations and wealthy individuals, after all, are only asking that organizations follow the same discipline that *they*—our prospects— have been practicing for years.

———————

Let's be clear: What we're talking about isn't the kind of "long-range planning" many institutions already do, but real strategic planning. The difference is important.

Traditional *long-range* planning is an administrative tool. Predictions are made on the basis of past performance, current resources and demographic trends.

Strategic planning is an entrepreneurial process. The organization attempts to *design* its own future— based on the external environment, its opportunities and constraints. Strategic planning looks at forces outside the organization's control, forces like rising expectations for health care or a declining industrial base.

Through this kind of planning, the organization examines its options; decides what its future directions *should* be; and develops an action plan, a budget and a timetable for meeting its objectives.

Any organization engaged in a structured development program also needs a written *fund-raising plan*. Again, the thinking of key volunteers is reflected in this plan, which is designed by a competent professional.

With these kinds of plans, an organization is seen as a quality operation—an intelligently managed enterprise, aware of its purpose and its environment, and ready to take advantage of opportunities as they arise. This kind of organization, in short, looks like a smart investment.

Without these plans, an organization remains one of thousands that struggle on from one year to the next, hoping to be able to continue to do what they've done before. In today's competitive environment, this kind of organization is a high risk.

If an organization has a valid mission and provides needed services, we *owe* it to those it serves to develop plans that will not only ensure its survival, but also provide for growth and change.

So don't wait until it's too late. Take a look around. Get the right kinds of people involved in your planning process. More than likely, they'll put their money on the plans they helped to build.

Share Your Plans
Without Asking for Money

A campaign with untested goals and unidentified leaders is a campaign that is not in your best interest.

Through your planning process, you've decided what your financial objectives ought to be. Now, to find out *if* the funds can be raised—and *how* they can be raised—it's essential that you share your plans with the donor community.

How do you go about getting an accurate reading without submitting to "trial by fire"—that is, without actually asking for the money?

The standard procedure is to conduct a feasibility study—discussed in the following pages. Another is the cultivation or "awareness" program.

Sitting across from a fund-raising executive at a meeting one day was an estate planner. At a similar meeting at lunch the next day, an attorney and an accountant were in attendance. These people were on hand to take part in a series of small-group meetings being sponsored by the community's largest hospital.

The purpose was to address several major health care issues, and to discuss the hospital's plans for responding to these issues. The hospital was intent on getting the benefit of the guests' thinking.

These meetings were designed primarily for major prospects. While our three professionals could make significant gifts in their own right, the real reason for inviting them was that they were counsellors to the best prospects in the community.

Little did anyone know, however, that they would come to play such an important role in the hospital's development program. For they turned out to be the three major advisors for one of the hospital's top prospects.

This prospect also attended one of the meetings. Later, with his three advisors, he worked out a plan that resulted in a $1 million commitment to the hospital.

What made this series of meetings especially effective was their dual purpose: not only to provide information, but also to obtain the views of the guests. In this way, the fund-raising program could be built in concert with their concerns and interests.

From the institution's perspective, such a series of meetings might be called a "cultivation" program. For marketing purposes, "leadership awareness program" is more appealing.

The idea is to share the organization's plans in an unpretentious, small-group setting, with plenty of time for reactions, questions and discussion. No funds are solicited, and no one is asked to volunteer—but a lot can be accomplished.

This process can give an organization what one executive calls a "reality fix." That is, you'll find out what the leaders in your community think of your organization and its fund-raising plans, and what concerns and problems you'll need to deal with.

The traditional cultivation program is most often used to help an organization find out whether it can attain a certain financial objective. But such a program can tell you much more. In fact, you can determine *how* to reach your goal, based on a knowledge of the donor community and specific donors—as well as the dynamics that might be brought into play between Donor A and Donor B.

These are the kinds of insights that can help you put together an effective fund-raising strategy.

And there's another benefit: For people to be able to provide informed responses, they will usually recognize that they need to know about your organization and its plans (however tentative).

Because of their need to know, they're likely to be receptive listeners. This gives you an excellent opportunity to briefly present your case—test market it, if you will—at a time when funds are not being solicited, and when their thinking can influence your own.

This approach seeks to cultivate relationships with donors by *involving* them—the best kind of cultivation. There are other ways that can also be effective.

One method is direct mail. This vehicle can be used to provide information through a series of letters or publications; or to solicit memberships or small contributions. The purpose is to stimulate interest and to attract new donors, some of whom may become major prospects down the line.

Another method of cultivation includes all the activities that come under the heading of public relations. These include news coverage in the print and broadcast media; editorials; public service advertising;

a speakers' bureau for community groups and organizations; and benefits and special events.

The primary advantage of these activities is that they keep your organization's good work in the public eye—most importantly the eye of your *prospect*. They are not a substitute for face-to-face cultivation activities that promote dialogue. But they can help. They can create a favorable climate for raising money.

Use a Feasibility Study to Build a Strategy

Once people have helped us to shape our development plans, we need to ask them what they are willing to *do* to help transform the plans into realities.

The courteous and elegant way to find out this kind of information—without "putting the arm" on anyone—is to conduct a series of *confidential,* one-on-one interviews.

This process, called a feasibility or market study, is usually carried out by a consultant. The reason is that a consultant, as an "outsider," can expect candid, straightforward answers—and provide an objective analysis of the results.

Some practitioners are wedded to the more limited and traditional purpose of the study: to test the feasibility of reaching the dollar goal, period.

But a study can do much more than this. It's a very effective way to *listen to and involve* people who will be crucial to the success of the program.

With the information and insights gained through the study, we can begin to build an overall *strategy* for the campaign. Equally important, we can start to think in term of specific *tactics*—that is, how to best approach a certain prospect.

For the study provides a golden opportunity to learn each prospect's attitude toward the organization and its plans. Within the total program, which projects does the prospect favor, and why? Is the prospect likely to contribute to one of these projects? Is he or she likely to become a volunteer solicitor? A campaign leader?

A feasibility study enables us to get the answers "from the horse's mouth," so to speak. By ensuring confidentiality and placing an outside consultant in charge, we create an atmosphere where people can speak freely.

A study can tell us whether the organization is ready to embark on a program. We can find out what people consider to be the strengths and weaknesses of the case and program. We can identify prospects for pace-setting contributions, and often learn what they think.

The study, in fact, can be seen as "the first call for money"—the first step in the marketing of the upcoming campaign. In a quiet, dignified way, the study puts people on alert. It can even start the wheels turning.

A few years ago, an Illinois hospital conducted a study to determine the feasibility of a $2.8 million campaign. Among those interviewed in the small town was the president of its largest company.

During the interview, the company president was shown a "standards chart" which indicated the size and number of commitments—based on past experience—that would be required to raise $2.8 million.

The top investment would have to be $500,000.

"Although I'm not seeking a commitment," said the interviewer, "I do need your opinion on whether these standards can be achieved. Do you see your company as being among the top five gifts on the chart?"

"Yes," the executive answered, "but the validity of these standards is critical." He kept prodding: "Are you sure these figures are reliable? Can we raise $2.8 million without reaching these standards?"

At the time, the interviewer wasn't sure exactly *why* this gentleman was so concerned with the levels of investment that would be required. He did reassure the company president that the standards *were* an accurate predictor of success.

———————

While the interviewer was finishing his study and writing his report, the company president went to work behind the scenes to line up the necessary support within his firm for a $500,000 pledge. All this took

41

place before it had even been determined that the hospital could conduct a successful campaign.

Three months before the campaign was announced, the company confirmed that the hospital could count on a $500,000 commitment. The hospital went on to raise its $2.8 million—ahead of schedule.

What was remarkable about this experience is that the very *process* of conducting the feasibility study may have done more for the success of the campaign than did all the information that was obtained, and all the strategy that was built upon it.

It's not unusual for this kind of thing to happen when an organization involves the right people in its plans for development. What's important is for us to *hear* those people who can make our program work. The way we go about it (through a strategic planning process, a cultivation program or a formal feasibility study) is secondary.

In the final analysis, if you've given your prospects some kind of opportunity to tell you what they want—and especially if you've responded to their interests—you'll be in a strong position to develop a sense of commitment to your program.

We couldn't say it any better than Aldous Huxley did: "It's not very difficult to persuade people to do what they already long to do."

III

Setting the Pace
for Giving

*If the most capable give substantially
and give early, the others will follow—
as night follows day.*

If You Seek Average Gifts,
You Get Below-Average Results

You can't jump across a chasm in two equal leaps
and expect to have any followers.

People inexperienced in fund raising often think in
terms of "average" gifts. They have somehow gotten it
into their heads that what you do is divide the goal by
the number of likely donors, then ask everyone to give
the same amount.

For example, if the goal is $1 million, and there are
200 good prospects, someone will suggest that each
prospect be asked for $5,000. The idea is to reach the
goal through 100 per cent participation at the $5,000
level.

Assuming that everyone can easily afford to give
$5,000, this sounds like it should make the volunteer's
job easier. But seeking average gifts produces below-
average results. In fact, it is certain to lead to failure.

One problem with raising money by the multiplica-
tion table—$5,000 times 200—is that not everyone will
participate. We'd like to think they will, but they
won't. Even worse, seeking $5,000 from each donor

will, in effect, set a ceiling on what an inspired donor may want to pledge.

Tolstoy described this phenomenon in *War and Peace:* "The distinguished dignitary who bore the title of 'Collector of Alms' went round to all the brothers. Pierre would have liked to subscribe all he had, but, fearing that it might look like pride, subscribed the same amount as the others."

Let's say someone you know pledges $5,000. You feel that because of the donor's financial circumstances, he or she is twice as capable as you. Are *you* likely to pledge $5,000? We all tend to give in relation to what others are giving.

"One hundred per cent participation" has a nice ring to it, but doesn't work much better than seeking average gifts. When the word gets out that the objective is to get *everyone* to give, no matter how much, many people will give as little as they can. This tokenism will lower the sights of the leaders, and you'll raise less money.

Finally, the "averaging" approach assumes that twenty pledges of $5,000 each, taken together, will have the same impact as a single pledge of $100,000. Not so. In fund raising, the commitment that really counts is not the average one or the token one. It's the *leadership* commitment that makes things happen.

A Few Will Do the Most

"What's the status of our top ten?"

Anyone who has worked with a first-rate fund-raising professional knows well the sound of these words. For the most successful people in this business are known for focusing on the few who will do the most—the small number of prospects who will produce the greatest results.

The professionals know from experience that in most programs, ninety per cent of the funds come from about ten per cent of the donors.

This interesting phenomenon seems to be almost universal. People in sales often say that ninety per cent of their dollar volume comes from ten per cent of their customers.

Just as the salesman spends most of his time on his big customers, we devote most of our efforts to the major donors. We need to ask again and again, "What's the status of our top ten?" For what these folks do is going to make or break the campaign.

From studying the giving patterns of past campaigns, we've learned a lot more about how many will have to give how much in order to attain the goal. To help direct the energies of volunteers, this wisdom is typically set forth on a single sheet full of numbers—numbers whose significance can hardly be overstated.

This document, the "standards chart" or "table of investments," lists the number of contributions at various levels that have been found to be necessary to reach the goal.

For example, most successful $1 million campaigns have had a top commitment of $100,000, or ten per cent. Typically, you also have to secure something in the range of one contribution at the $75,000 level; two at the $50,000 level; three at $25,000; and three at $15,000. These ten commitments total $395,000 or 39.5 per cent of the goal.

The next 100 commitments should account for another thirty or forty per cent of the goal; "numerous others" will generate the balance.

This is called the "rule of the thirds." To wit: One-third of the goal is usually raised from each group—the top ten, the next 100 and everybody else.

The rule, of course, is applied with some flexibility. The numbers on the standards chart are adjusted somewhat, according to the type of organization and the giving history of the community. In some cases, the top donor may have to get you 20 per cent of the way home, and the top ten may have to contribute fifty to sixty per cent of the total.

The standards chart also helps you figure out how many people will have to be solicited. Normally, to secure each commitment, you'll need two to four prospects.

If you know how many prospects you need, it's easy to get from there to the number of volunteers you should enlist. Divide the total number of prospects by five. This assumes that the volunteers themselves will be prospects, and that each will call on four others— which is probably the most you'll want to assign to anyone.

Where will you find your best prospects? Experience shows that the best prospects for the immediate future are those who have given in the past. "Remember that the best prospects are those who have already given," said Si Seymour, "and that the more a person gives, the more likely he is to give more."

New givers, of course, are always necessary in order to replenish the pool of contributors. But concentrate your efforts on the few who will do the most. Then you'll have the luxury of broadening your base—the "grassroots" donors who will someday become your new top ten.

The Early Donor Sets the Pace

"He who gives early gives twice."

—Cervantes

The point is not that he who gives early should immediately be asked to give again—but that his or her contribution can *set an example* for others to follow.

If those who give early also give at the higher levels, so much the better. Major commitments that are made late in the campaign are wonderful, but they don't have the same pace-setting power. There's no chance for them to *communicate*.

This is what makes the beginning of the campaign a time of special opportunity.

Let's say that the first contribution to a campaign comes in at $2,000—instead of the $1,000 that was expected. The next person to make a commitment may well give $1,500—instead of the $750 he or she was considering. This can create a ripple effect that carries through the ranks.

Of course, a "negative ripple effect" can also occur. If the first contribution comes in at $500, instead of the anticipated $1,000, then the next person might decide to give only $250, rather than $500.

In either case, it's the people who give first who set the pattern for those who follow. So it pays to devote a lot of thought to the order in which they are approached.

———————

Ben Franklin's two hundred year-old formula for success has held up so well that one campaign director we know makes a point of quoting it to every group of volunteers he works with:

"My practice," explained Franklin, "is to go first to those who may be counted upon to be favorable, who know the cause and believe in it, and ask them to give as generously as possible. When they have done so, I go next to those who may be presumed to have a favorable opinion and to be disposed to listening, and secure their adherence.

"Lastly, I go to those who know little of the matter or have no known predilection for it and influence

50

them by presentation of the names of those who have already given."

Our voluntary organizations still follow this advice. But now we structure our programs so that the very first people we see are those who are not only the *closest* to the cause—but also the most likely to contribute at the *highest levels,* relative to their capacity.

The first people to be solicited are often grouped into a "pacesetters" or "advance gifts" division. This group includes prospects at various levels who have been selected because we expect that they will serve as examples for their peers.

How moving and inspiring it can be when a custodian on the college staff pledges $5,000 to "his" school. Certainly, this kind of sacrifice can motivate others in circumstances like his. But it can also set an example for others with a greater capacity who hear about the custodian's commitment. They'll see it as the best evidence that this school is loved and worth investing in.

So first, identify people who are likely to make commitments that are large for their financial circumstances. Solicit these folks before anyone else, so the news of their commitments will encourage the rest to join in. Those who stepped to the forefront will then have the reward of watching others follow their lead.

Trustees Have an Opportunity, Not an Obligation

Other donors will always look to the trustees to set the process in motion. People will always ask, and with good reason: "What did the board do?"

Whatever example the board sets, the effect will be felt throughout the enterprise. "As the board goes," according to the old saying, "so goes the campaign."

This does not mean, however, that the trustees should be pressured. How dismaying it is to hear, "It's the rent you pay for the space you take"—or, "It's give, get or get off."

Trusteeship presents an *opportunity,* not an obligation. The trustee's commitment is voluntary. It is an expression of leadership.

The trustee carries the torch of voluntarism and lights the path for others. James F. Oates, former chairman of the Equitable Life Assurance Society of the United States, made it clear: "The trustees have to lead in acts and deeds, as well as in words and titles."

After serving as general chairman of a successful campaign for Princeton University, Mr. Oates said, "I think if I had to select the one most important decision we made during this campaign, it was the decision that we would not publicly announce it or start it until every trustee—*every trustee*—had made a substantial, sacrificial gift. You can't expect to have a following without that leadership."

The same kind of opportunity presents itself to those who provide voluntary leadership for the fund-raising program—who may or may not be trustees. This group, the "campaign cabinet" or "campaign executive committee," includes those who will be asking others to give. They have an excellent opportunity to lead the way by their deeds.

But from the ranks of the trustees and the campaign cabinet, a dangerous idea may be expressed. Someone is likely to ask, "If a person can *raise* a lot of money, isn't that person valuable—even if his or her personal gift isn't much?"

Not really. First, the person who asks another to make a greater sacrifice than he or she has made is not setting the best kind of precedent. Second, and even more importantly, this person is investing time and energy in the campaign—but without exercising the *maximum influence* at his or her disposal. The volunteer who solicits others without the benefit of a strong personal example is like the shoemaker who goes without shoes.

It's certainly easy enough to understand, however, why many trustees are reluctant donors—and why many boards fail to set a strong example as a group.

Some organizations enlist trustees without regard for their affluence and influence. There's nothing wrong with enlisting a trustee because of the constituency that person represents, or because of the special expertise he or she can bring to the board. But we shouldn't expect fund-raising miracles from this kind of trustee.

Other organizations *do* enlist people who have the capacity to contribute and to raise money. But then the organization fails to involve them or give them anything meaningful to do—until it's campaign time.

Trustees need to have an important role in the organization. They need a chance to develop their rightful sense of ownership. Members of a "rubber-stamp" board may well think of fund raising as an administrative function. Don't be surprised if they aren't responsive to lofty rhetoric about "leadership" when there's money to be raised.

Staff Giving Lends Credibility

"Why bother to solicit the staff? There's not much money in it, is there?"

Maybe not—but if the staff has an opportunity to give, and responds at a high level in relation to their capacity, you've gained much more than dollars.

First, staff contributions can have a powerful impact on the rest of your donor constituency.

Together with the trustees and other volunteer groups, the staff is part of the "official family" of the organization. Their commitment provides others with a clear indication that those who are most intimate with the organization—those who see it every day—*do* believe in its value and respect its leadership. Through their actions, they attest to the wisdom of the development effort.

There's another benefit that may be even more important to the future of the organization. A museum curator once told me, "I think our involvement is very good for staff spirit. We feel like we're a part of the development effort—that we're helping to make this museum an even better place to work."

An intensive fund-raising effort is most successful when it is a *total effort* of the organization. A campaign presents an opportunity for everyone in the official family to become involved in building the organization's future—to become an "ambassador for development." Everyone who will benefit from the success of the program deserves a chance to invest in it and to work for it.

Too often, however, the staff isn't approached in this spirit. Instead, they're made to feel that their involvement is a requirement, rather than an opportunity. As employees, they may feel that their jobs, salaries or promotions may be at stake.

That kind of approach will backfire every time. In asking anyone for money, but especially the staff, we must take seriously the premise that giving is *voluntary*. Otherwise, we may succeed in raising money, but we won't have succeeded in winning friends. In the long run, that's no success at all, is it?

Make Great Investments Possible

Not long ago, a prominent family in a Northern industrial city made a $2 million commitment to the city's leading university.

The impact of this kind of investment can hardly be measured. In this case, it was the largest philanthropic investment ever made in that part of the state. Many people asked, "How did they manage to give so much?"

The fact is that if the pledge had to be paid in cash, the family might never have done it. The investment was made possible by a combination of several devices—including a subscription period and the use of financial vehicles other than cash.

How can these kinds of ideas be used in your program?

● Provide prospects flexible payment terms through a *subscription period*. This will allow them to spread the payments, and the tax benefits, over a period of years. In this way, the donor can often make a larger commitment.

A person or a company that can write a check for $50,000 can usually pledge $150,000 over a three-year period. Trustees are often offered a five-year pledge period, and we're beginning to see commitments made that will be fulfilled over a period of as much as ten years.

• Provide prospects with flexibility and choices in the *financial vehicle* they can use to make their commitments. Certain instruments (appreciated securities, trusts, real estate or insurance policies) can have distinct tax advantages. These more creative vehicles can also enable donors to hold the assets or retain the income to provide for their own security.

Tax savings are rarely the major motivation for donors. Once the decision to contribute has been made, however, the savings can allow the donor to make a greater commitment at less actual cost.

• Provide prospects with recognition through a program of *named commemorative opportunities.* Such a program offers tangible and public recognition for major investments—through the naming of physical facilities, scholarships and the like.

Commemorative opportunities are used to suggest a particular level of investment, and often to "raise the sights" of the donor. For example, instead of asking the prospect for a commitment of $140,000, it is suggested that for $150,000, some program or project can be named in honor of the prospect, his or her family, another individual, or a corporation.

Such a proposal is best received when it is tailored to the interests of the donor.

A variation on this theme is the use of *giving clubs* in annual programs. (No, that's not what you hit someone with to get them to give.) Several clubs are created for those who contribute at different levels. Those who increase their commitments move up into the more prestigious clubs. Those at the top levels may receive such benefits as an annual dinner with the chief executive officer, or special access to the institution's facilities and services.

• Provide donors with opportunities for *planned giving*. Together with capital campaigns and annual programs, planned (or "deferred") giving has become one of the three basic supports for the philanthropic tripod.

By arranging for a deferred payment, usually to be made after death, the donor is often able to make a greater commitment than he or she ever would have expected.

The old adage, "He who advocates must first bequeath," is becoming more of a reality. This effort, like most others, is best led by example; when trustees do it, others will follow.

Cultivate trust officers, accountants and attorneys so that they will be receptive to the idea of planned giving, and willing to provide the necessary technical assistance. But rely on the development staff to inform the appropriate prospects about the benefits of planned giving, and to attract them to the program.

Use these various tools, separately or in combination, to make it easier for donors to do the great things they want to do. If there's a will, so to speak, there's probably a way.

IV

Applying
the Campaign Principle

*Structure makes people more productive.
It gives them standards against which
they can measure their performance.*

People Prefer Structure

Asking people to work in an "unstructured" setting is like sending them out to hunt polar bears in a snowstorm.

If you want people to be effective, you have to give them a structure. There has to be a way to measure performance and results—something against which to shine.

Human beings need goals and deadlines. They need to know what is expected of them, and where they fit into the big picture.

The person responsible for directing the program has to provide the volunteers with this kind of structure.

This is especially critical because campaign management is *project* management. It calls for building an organization to accomplish a specific purpose over a limited period of time.

We can't just pull together a bunch of people and turn them loose with pledge cards. Organizations that use this approach (and there are more than a few) end up with a demoralized group of volunteers, a floundering campaign and a poor reputation in the community. It should come as no surprise that ambiguous plans produce ambiguous results.

For example, volunteers should be asked to assume definite and limited jobs. The way to enlist a busy community leader is to hand him or her a job description—a list of four or five tasks that need to be accomplished, along with a timetable.

The way *not* to enlist that leader is to say, "Well, we need X thousand dollars, and we'd like you to help out. There won't be a lot of meetings, though—just a couple of cards." People with fund-raising experience know where that leads. The others will soon find out.

Most of the nitty-gritty work of a campaign is accomplished through committees. But people shouldn't be enlisted by asking them to join a committee. One of the best enlistments I ever heard went like this: "Because you're a leader in this community, I feel that you, as I do, have a sense of obligation—really a sense of opportunity—to do this important job."

For people to work effectively within our structure, we also have to create a *positive climate*—a climate of optimism, enthusiasm and confidence. Without this kind of atmosphere, assignments and deadlines are useless.

Good things rarely happen in a bad atmosphere. Once in a while, someone will express the idea that people will perform better if we tell them how badly things are going. That's the wrong approach to management, especially the management of volunteers.

We want to give people the same sense that Pogo, the comic strip character, did when he proclaimed: "We're faced with insurmountable opportunity."

In short, we don't try to coerce people into performing. We build a structure to direct people; to channel their energies; to bring out the *best* in them.

Take One Step at a Time

"Nothing is particularly hard," said Henry Ford, "if you divide it into small jobs."

The task of building 100,000 cars—or raising a million dollars—can appear staggering, until it is broken down into a series of small and logical steps.

This is an excellent reason for placing *one professional* in charge of managing a fund-raising program—someone who has the overview, knows the steps and can direct the volunteers.

"A successful development effort results from a series of steps, taken one at a time, each done in correct sequence, according to a plan and schedule," explains James A. Jones, a consultant who has done in-depth studies of hundreds of campaigns.

"At any one time," says Mr. Jones, "people should be concerned with only one step. When a step is improperly taken, the next will be more difficult. When a step is correctly made, the next will be easier and more effective."

By taking one step at a time, you make the larger, more complex tasks manageable. You give your volunteers a fresh sense of accomplishment every day.

This rule applies on every level—from the assignments given to each volunteer to the major milestones in the overall progress of a campaign.

For example, each division (or group of prospects) needs to be solicited in sequence, to set the best possible pace for the effort. Prospects for six-figure contributions are solicited *before* five-figure prospects. In this way, the highest-level prospects will set the pattern for those who follow.

Even in soliciting a single prospect, there are critical steps to be taken in sequence. Before the prospect is solicited, he or she deserves to be informed about the *program*. And before the volunteer makes the call, he or she deserves to be informed about the *prospect*.

The proper pacing of a development program is both a science and an art. Volunteers often feel that the development officer or campaign director is moving too slowly. The professional often feels that the volunteers want to jump the gun. Depending on the situation, either may be right. That, it seems, is the way of the world.

Scheduling Creates Momentum

A fund-raising program has to be run a little like a kindergarten—with the idea that people's attention spans are limited.

This is no reflection on our volunteers; it's just a fact of life. The development professional has to be a bit of a master of ceremonies. He or she develops a schedule that keeps people fired up and excited, never allowing boredom to set in, and making sure the whole show is brought to a close before the audience gets tired.

How do you keep the excitement high? One principle to keep in mind is *synergy.*

Buckminster Fuller borrowed this term from metallurgy. If three metals, for example, are combined to form an alloy, the strength of the alloy can be greater than the sum of the strengths of the three component metals. Fuller extended this concept to any situation where, one might say, "the whole is greater than the sum of its parts."

A fund-raising campaign is one such situation. When three events—for example, three major commitments—happen at the same time, or in rapid succession, they can have a powerful impact on the campaign, far more than if the three events had occurred a couple of weeks apart. The point is that synergy gets people excited.

Something like this may happen by serendipity—

but as the veteran fund-raiser knows, nine times out of ten, it's all been carefully orchestrated in advance.

Scheduling events to create momentum calls for a lot of behind-the-scenes work. That means investing more resources in the development program. "The more time and money you have," says William Freyd of Institutional Development Counsel, "the more money you raise."

Once the curtain goes up and the program is announced, there is a rush of activity. For the campaign director, of course, the pace is often maddening to sustain. As Lewis Carroll observed:

". . . you see, it takes all the running you can do to keep in the same place. If you want to get somewhere else, you must run as least twice as fast as that!"

Build a Sense of Campaign

The winners of this world are those who set a goal, set a deadline, and place milestones along the way.

In campaigning, they ask people to serve in a hierarchy of leaders. They ask them to contribute to specific programs.

These are some of the hallmarks of a *campaign,* the greatest invention in fund raising since the bake sale. These are the structures and dynamics that will, in fact, enhance any development enterprise—and, for that matter, just about any human endeavor.

The dynamics that come into play during intense campaign activity can be truly exhilarating. Some people will even love the campaign more than the cause. It's anything but "business as usual."

To sustain the excitement, to keep the adrenalin flowing, is as necessary as it is nerve-wracking. Will we win? Oscar Wilde understood the ironic task of the campaign director: "The suspense is terrible. I hope it will last."

So cultivate the passions. Make them eager for the contest.

Create a Climate of Universality

"Public sentiment is everything. With public sentiment, nothing can fail. Without it, nothing can
succeed."

—Abraham Lincoln

Fund-raising programs prosper in a climate of universality. We can't force people to come to the show.
As Sol Hurok observed: "When people don't want to
come, nothing will stop them." But we *can* attract
them by organizing the effort in a way that makes it
most appealing.

One reason that the concept of a campaign works
so well is that everyone in the community joins in:
individuals, corporations, foundations, clubs, unions,
churches and even (praise be!) governments.

The more good people you can get into the parade,
the better. As one old campaigner used to say to me,
"You can't overwork the loyal few." Spread the work
among the largest possible group of *effective*
volunteers.

This will produce two results: An individual is
more likely to "join up," knowing that his or her load
will be manageable. And because more people get involved with the destiny of the institution, a sense of
universality will develop.

You may raise 90 per cent of your goal from a
handful of donors. But don't stop there. Give more
people a chance to get in on the action. Even if you

spend more than you raise in order to do this, the intangible benefits make it well worth the effort. Besides, the next time around, the little giver may become a big investor.

It's not a very good idea, though, to do as the chairman of a prominent school once did. He admonished his director of development to enlist three times as many volunteers as necessary—because he felt that when one or two didn't produce, the job might still get done.

The better way is not to enlist *any* laggards, if you can help it. They'll only drag everyone else down, and defeat the momentum and enthusiasm that's building.

Be selective. Enlist people who are known for coming through. Plan for the best in people, not the worst. What you plan for is what you're likely to get.

Winning Is Fundamental

You can't get results if you don't know where you're going. Set a dollar goal for your program—and set smaller goals along the way. Beware of the turtle who said, "I'm glad I'm going so slowly, because I'm not sure I'm headed in the right direction."

We all need to have objectives. "Before you can score," says a Greek proverb, "you must first have a goal."

The goal has to be high enough to stretch people, and low enough for them to reach. "When setting an objective for a campaign," says R. Blair Schreyer, president of Ketchum, Inc., "it is better to have a believable objective in which everyone has confidence. The probability is that you can oversubscribe a believable goal, but you will, almost without exception, undersubscribe an unbelievable goal."

Winning may not be everything. But you can't tell that to the winners of the world. A program that falls short of its goal may raise a lot of money, win new friends for an organization, and enable it to do more than before. But no team can *win* if it doesn't cross the goal line. "Close only counts in horseshoes."

Meetings Keep Things Moving

"Not *another* meeting!"

It's true—in every campaign, as in every other human enterprise, there are too many meetings. But that's because they *work*.

Meetings are the glue that keeps a fund-raising program together. Experience has shown that a person's effectiveness as a volunteer is directly related to his or her attendance at meetings.

Meetings accomplish a number of things:

- They provide opportunities to inform, stimulate, inspire and recognize people.
- They instill a positive, shared sense of responsibility among the people in attendance.
- They provide deadlines. To have something to talk about, you have to have *done* something. (We human beings will rarely accomplish that which we have plenty of time to accomplish.)

But how do you get people to *come*—so they can receive these fine benefits?

- Make sure the leaders treat the meeting as important.
- Start and stop on time.
- Always provide substance.
- If substance or attendance is lacking, postpone the meeting.

Meetings, of course, aren't the only way to get things done. If you use the other ways, too—the memo, the phone call, the personal visit—people are more likely to feel that any given meeting will be worth attending.

In the end, meetings have a lot to do with how people view the organization. Well-run and well-attended meetings provide tangible evidence of an effective organization and a strong fund-raising program.

V

Asking for Money

*The volunteer is an investment
counsellor—not a salesman.*

People Give to People

People don't give to an institution. They give to the person who asks them. Often, a contribution is made because of how one person feels about another. The institution may be almost incidental.

People also give *for* people—not for endowments or swimming pools.

Real money cannot be raised without people. At the outset of any campaign, someone will always say, "The money's out there." But the mere existence of money, without people to ask for it, is like a crop with no one to harvest it.

The donor, too, is *always* a person. A foundation, corporation or committee never makes a decision. Only people make decisions.

It is true, of course, that foundation proposals have to follow the foundation's guidelines. And a corporation needs a case that will justify its investment to stockholders.

But institutions don't submit proposals to boards of trustees; people submit proposals to people.

Once the volunteer and the prospect are together, the volunteer's own personal influence counts more than anything else. What the volunteer says to the prospect, and *how* he or she says it, will have the greatest impact on the outcome. Ultimately, the best tool of persuasion is the volunteer's own sincerity, interest and enthusiasm.

In other words, once the formalities are taken care of, the volunteer can act as the old saying advises: "Words that come from the heart enter the heart."

John D. Rockefeller, Jr. said it all (it took him a few words, to do it, but they're worth reading):

"When a solicitor comes to you and lays on your heart the responsibility that rests so heavily on his; when his earnestness gives convincing evidence of how seriously interested he is; when he makes it clear that he knows you are no less anxious to do your duty in the matter than he is, that you are just as conscientious, that he feels sure all you need is to realize the importance of the enterprise and the urgency of the need in order to lead you to do your full share in meeting it—he has made you his friend and has brought you to think of giving not as a duty but as a privilege."

When we ask for money, we are friends, not adversaries. We are counsellors, not salesmen. It's not a game of predator and prey. We are trying to help the donor do something significant for the community and for society. After all, we're not asking for anything for ourselves.

Unfortunately, many institutions still think of fund raising as a "hard sell." They train a "sales force" and put them in the field with sales objectives, quotas and sales promotion literature. But major prospects—those who have been contributing large sums of money for a long time—will resist. They have become hardened to aggressive, manipulative selling.

The marketing approach is far more appropriate to the *people business* of fund raising. It's also more effective. This approach focuses on providing satisfaction and fulfillment for the donor, rather than getting the donor to take what the institution has to offer.

Businesses have found—and institutions are begining to discover—that if marketing is done first, then the sale comes easier. The "salesman" becomes an order-taker who helps the "consumer" make very human decisions and take delivery. The job is not to change a nay-sayer into a yea-sayer, but to increase an order or upgrade it. There's no need for begging or arm-twisting.

"The aim of marketing is to make selling superfluous," writes management consultant Peter Drucker. "The aim of marketing is to understand the customer so well that the product or service fits him and sells itself."

In this respect, philanthropy is not much different from business. People buy from companies, invest in them and work for them because they feel that the enterprise can satisfy their human needs and desires, and because they believe in the *people* who represent the enterprise.

The Right Person
Makes the Difference

What is the secret of fund-raising success?

Many a veteran will say, "Select the right person to ask the right person, in the right way, for the right amount, for the right reason, at the right time."

This old maxim of fund raising still holds true—although it's a little mysterious. It's like that sure-fire formula for making a bundle in the stock market: "Only buy stocks that are going up."

Both these pieces of advice point you in the right direction, but don't tell you how to get there. The "how" depends on circumstance and opportunity—the kind of realities that require the judgment of a seasoned professional.

People who are experienced at assessing these situations will usually insist on holding out for the "right person" to call on a certain prospect. They know that prospective donors are just plain more receptive if they're asked by someone they respect. In practice, this usually means a peer or someone at a higher level of influence.

Often, it's not a question of the "right person," but of the "right people"—a team of two working together. As it is written in the Talmud, "If two logs are dry and one is wet, the kindling of the two will kindle the wet one, too."

The order in which a volunteer sees his or her prospects is important, too. The prospect that should be seen first is the one considered most likely to come through at the suggested level. The success of this first call can help in subsequent calls on other prospects.

The whole idea is to be *strategic*. The campaign director or the chief development officer, if he or she is a good listener, is in the best position to be the primary strategist.

The One Who Asks Must First Give

He: You know, you ought to get some of that company's stock. They're really going places.

She: Really? How much did you buy?

He: Oh, I didn't buy any yet. I'm planning to. I just think it's a good idea for you.

In business or in philanthropy, a person's actions are more convincing than his or her advice. There's nothing wrong with good advice and good intentions—but the force of example is more compelling. In practice, a leader is one who expresses convictions through actions.

This is the cardinal rule of fund raising: A volunteer must make a *personal commitment* before asking others. That is a given.

To be even more effective, the volunteer will want to give at the proper level. That level should be no less, according to the volunteer's means, than what the prospect is being asked to do.

As Socrates counselled: "Let him that would move the world first move himself."

See Each Prospect Face to Face

If we really believe that people are more important than dollars, then we owe it to our top prospects to visit them in person. Besides, seeing people face to face *works* better than any other method.

In philanthropy, as in friendship, the letter and the telephone can get things started—or keep them going—but the *real* relationship is built in person. Nothing says you care like being there.

The prospect should be called on the phone only to set up an appointment. The danger is being drawn into soliciting by long distance. If this happens, the prospect will never know how willing we were to take the time for a personal visit.

The plan for a broad-based campaign may call for soliciting smaller gifts by telephone, mail or even television. Even here, the more personal we can get, the

80

better the results will be. We can use the telephone script to provide a framework, but we should *listen* to the prospect. It needs to be a conversation, not a sales pitch. When we write a letter to 10,000 people, it's most effective to write for just *one* person.

The same principle applies when recruiting volunteers: Get as personal as you can. Always enlist a person *in* person.

Ask for a Specific Amount; Ask for Enough

Most prospective donors want some guidance— the more specific, the better. "Whatever you can do" is a recipe for failure. It suggests that the organization is ambiguous about the whole enterprise.

Again, John D. Rockefeller, Jr. spoke for most donors: ". . . I do like a man to say to me, 'We are trying to raise $4 million, and are hoping you may be desirous of giving ____ dollars. If you see your way clear to do so, it will be an enormous help and encouragement. You may have it in mind to give more; if so, we shall be glad. On the other hand, you may feel you cannot give as much, in view of other responsibilities. If that is the case, we shall understand."

Many volunteers are also surprised to learn that prospects prefer to be asked for *enough*: enough to reflect their stature and capability, and enough to really get the job done. Prospects, once motivated to contribute, are likely to be embarrassed by a request to give *less* than they're able—rather than by a request to give more.

Don't follow the example set by a famous neurological institute when they asked their doctors to bequeath their brains for research. They ended their appeal with the traditional line: "Any contribution, however small, will be gratefully appreciated."

If they're going to be associated with a program, most people genuinely want to make investments that will help to ensure its success. Many donors would agree with the sentiment expressed by a friend many years ago: "Don't give until it hurts. Give until it feels good."

It's easier to "feel good" if we have something against which to measure our performance. That's why specificity—a high degree of specificity—tends to be most effective in raising funds.

Qualify the Prospect

What you ask a particular prospect to give should be based on what he or she *could* give—if properly motivated and asked by the right person. The key is what the prospect is *capable of*, not what you think he or she is likely to do.

Rather than saying, "This is what we have you down for," the figure is presented as a suggested guide-line—a "think about" figure. It's proportional to what others in similar financial circumstances are being asked to consider.

How do you determine what to ask for?

The best way is to organize an anonymous committee of peers—a prospect evaluation committee. This group studies the standards chart (the number of contributions at each level that will be necessary to reach the goal), and tries to decide which prospects are capable of investing at these levels.

For the suggested asking figures to be effective, serious thought should be given to the membership of this committee. Certainly, you want people who are aware of other people's means. But you'll be a step ahead if you include those who are likely to become part of the program's leadership. They'll be able to defend their evaluations, if need be, and their own sights may well be raised by participating in this process.

It's been proven time and again: If the people who

will be responsible for asking for money have had a good deal to say about *how much* will be asked for, from whom and for what, then the program has a better chance to succeed.

Of course, in prospect evaluations, confidentiality is the rule. We don't want to infringe on people's privacy. But we *do* want to make sure that our energies are concentrated on those prospects who have the capacity to make the program a reality. It's unfair to ask a volunteer to "aim high" without providing enough information about the prospect.

Evaluations are based primarily on what we learn *from the prospect* directly, and also on what we learn about the prospect from his or her peers. Research by the development staff, using public record information, can help to fill in the picture.

Various methods can be brought into play when setting asking figures. One medical center, for example, looked at the percentage of the goal that each corporate prospect contributed to the last campaign, nine years earlier. (If you use this method, remember that many things can change with time—a corporation's capacity and willingness to give, its priorities, its leadership and its relationships with organizations.)

In a university campaign, another formula was used to establish the "think about" figure: a simple $500 per employee. Sales or net income, if they can be learned, may provide more equitable standards. But we have to be careful not to turn voluntary giving into something that looks like taxation.

Sectors of the corporate community, such as the banks or the insurance companies, may decide to give a certain percentage of the goal as a group. Many companies relate their giving to what the biggest company in town does, or consult informally with each other during the "think about" period.

However prospects are evaluated, there are two other determinations that should be made in advance.

The first is to *qualify* your prospects and separate them from mere "suspects."

A qualified prospect must have the *financial capability.* He or she should have some *rationale for giving* to the program—a philosophical rationale, if not active interest or involvement in the organization. And he or she should have some *history of giving*—to other organizations, if not to your own. It's very difficult to turn a non-giver into a giver.

A second critical determination is the *pathway* to the prospect. Unless someone has access to the prospect, he or she is still a "suspect." In so many communities, the out-of-town consultant is told: "There's a lot of money in this community." The consultant, with good reason, will usually respond: "That's great. Now who's going to go out and ask for it?"

Prospect evaluation is a sensitive and time-consuming process, but an absolutely essential one. Those who put in long hours as anonymous members of the evaluation committee are among the unsung heroes of fund raising. Without them, few campaigns would succeed.

Tenacity Prevails

"Let me tell you the secret that has led me to my goal," said Louis Pasteur. "My strength lies solely in my tenacity."

The playwright Noel Coward agreed: "Thousands of people have talent. I might as well congratulate you for having eyes in your head. The one and only thing that counts is: Do you have staying power?"

Let's face it: Before a commitment can be secured from a prospect, a volunteer may have to call on the person two, three or four times. As the old fund-raising adage says, "You can't make a good pickle overnight, just by squirting a little vinegar on a cucumber. It takes a while."

And so it is with a meaningful commitment. It will almost always take more than one visit to provide the necessary "soaking time."

There are a couple of techniques to keep in mind. First, if the prospect is dubious or hasn't made a decision yet, it's probably unwise to rush him or her into a premature "no"—or a token gift. It's better to give the prospect some time to think it over, and give yourself some time to strategize.

The volunteer may spend the first visit or two just providing information, answering questions—being a good *investment counsellor*. The "order" may not even be asked for until the prospect appears ready to place it. Perhaps the volunteer will come back with another to assist, or a new idea to motivate the prospect—such as a commemorative opportunity or a creative financial vehicle.

If you happen to be that volunteer, you will almost certainly need more than one visit. Just make sure that before you leave the prospect, you have a definite appointment to return.

And whatever you do, don't get discouraged. Remember, even Babe Ruth struck out 1,330 times.

Ask for the Order

Without the invitation to invest, there's not likely to be a commitment.

Every experienced fund raiser has a personal version of the old story: A major commitment comes from an unexpected source. When the donor is asked why he or she never gave before, the answer is, "Because nobody ever asked me."

Some donors, of course, prefer to offer, rather than to be asked—especially if "asking" means the old-fashioned "hard sell." Philanthropist Albert Ratner of Cleveland is one:

"I'll kick out of my office anyone who comes and says, 'I've got you down for such-and-such an amount.'

"Instead," says Mr. Ratner, "the solicitor should tell me about the program, about the plans and about his interest in them. Then, at the end of the discussion, I will naturally ask him how I can help, how much I can give and what good that amount of money will do."

In philanthropy, clearly, a premature discussion of money is no better than the car salesman telling you the price before showing you the car. But where most of us go wrong is in waiting *too* long. Too many times, the volunteer leaves the prospect without having "asked for the order."

Words more enduring than these have not been written: "Ask, and it shall be given you; seek, and ye shall find."

A more contemporary sage, Will Rogers, put it this way: "Even if you're on the right track, you'll get run over if you just sit there." We can do our research; we can cultivate, involve and enlist. But if we don't move ahead and ask, we've missed our opportunity.

VI

Practicing Stewardship

*The task is not to get a donation–
but to develop a donor.*

The Donor Deserves
Good Stewardship

In business, the objective is not to make a sale, but to make a customer. In philanthropy, the objective is not to secure a donation, but to *develop a donor.*

Our job is not finished when the solicitations are completed, the commitments made, and the goal achieved. That's when the task of stewardship *begins.*

Good stewardship means protecting and managing the donor's investment—so that it produces the best possible return. It means using the money as the donor intended it to be used.

The National 4-H Council believes so strongly in this principle that it provides donors with a signed agreement that specifies what the organization will do in exchange for the donor's investment.

Good stewardship also means *thanking* the contributor. We owe it to donors to recognize their deeds. As Seneca wrote, "There is as much greatness of mind in acknowledging a good turn, as in doing it." Moreover, it's in the organization's own best interest to express its thanks. As it's often said, the first step in attracting the next investment is acknowledging the last.

A "thank you" note should be sent on the same day as the contribution is received. But it's not enough to send a form letter, hang a plaque or issue a bulletin. It has to be a personal letter, a personal call, a personal visit.

And it's not enough to express gratitude only once. "Go often to the house of thy friend," advises an old Scandinavian proverb, " for weeds soon choke up the unused path." Report to the donor the benefits that have come from his or her investment.

If donors only hear from us when we're asking for money, they'll be less likely to respond. Build ongoing relationships with your contributors. Invite them. Recognize them. Involve them. Ask them. Send them information before others receive it.

The principles of good stewardship apply to the way we treat volunteers, as well as donors. The people who raise the money deserve our thanks and recognition. We need to stay in touch with them, to keep them involved. By leaving someone on the shelf, we aren't "saving" them for later; we're distancing ourselves from them and letting the relationship slide.

In a way, stewardship begins as soon as a volunteer joins the team. We need to do everything we can to give the volunteer a good experience. The better that experience, the more likely it is that he or she will want to *stay* with the organization. That's important, because the most successful organizations are those that are best able to attract and retain volunteers.

If it seems that good stewardship will use up a lot of energy, it will. One way to look at it is to consider stewardship a "cost of doing business." One YMCA appropriates a small percentage of the dollars it raises toward this cost.

Good stewardship is well worth the extra effort it requires. It is the bedrock on which the future of an organization is built.

VII

Kindling the Spirit
of Philanthropy

*Inspire the best people to become your
best advocates.*

The Best Advocate
Is Both Donor and Volunteer

In the art and science of philanthropy, when all is said and done, our mission is this: to inspire the best people to become our best advocates.

The best advocates inspire others by the force of example. The advocate gives and asks others to give; works and asks others to work.

These are four aspects of the same impulse—the philanthropic spirit. In our urge to make fund raising more specialized, more professional, more sophisticated, we should never lose sight of this essential and beautiful simplicity.

"What it's all about," says one veteran trustee, "is asking the most respected and successful people: "if you believe in this cause, as I do, will you make as large an investment in it as you can, and will you ask another to do the same?"

All the ideas and techniques described in this book spring from this dynamic: inviting others to join together with us in doing important things. Everything

97

we do in the course of raising money, we do to facilitate this process, to help it unfold—for the benefit of the cause, the donor, the community, the nation.

In the business of raising money, we cannot allow ourselves to become mere technicians or manipulators. Certainly, we can never go back to being beggars or predators. We should never feel ashamed or apologize for what we do.

Our mission is to provide people with opportunities to do great things . . . to challenge and inspire them . . . to involve them in enterprises that will make life better for our generation, and future generations— enterprises that will advance our civilization as only voluntary action can.

If we can succeed in this, we won't have to be too concerned about raising money. For we will have succeeded in kindling the spirit of philanthropy.

A Word on
Fund-Raising Professionals
and Consultants

*Fund-raising expertise can be an
investment, rather than an expense.*

Hire the Best—
and Let Them Direct

Trustees and their chief executives are well advised to hire the best development professionals they can attract. If they do, the trustees won't get caught up in managing the fund-raising program. They'll be free to focus their energies where they'll be most effective —using their influence with peers.

It's a simple equation. When the professional's fund-raising knowledge and management skills are combined with the volunteer's influence, the result is success.

The development officer, in most cases, should not be expected to personally solicit contributions or recruit volunteers. The high-quality development officer should be expected to see that these things *are* done, and done well.

What makes a good development officer?

• The effective development executive has finely-tuned *interpersonal skills*. The basic question is: Can he or she inspire the kind of confidence that will draw people to the program?

The senior development officer who does not form close working relationships with the CEO and the trustees won't be able to accomplish very much. This officer has to be able to direct their activities with respect to development.

He or she needs to become accepted as the insistent voice for the basic principles and techniques of the field. In most situations, the professional is expected to provide formal training in those principles and techniques for the trustees and volunteers.

• The best development professionals are *strategists*. They can be expected to provide a detailed fundraising plan—including objectives, policies, procedures, organization, timetable and budget. It's not unusual to hear the executive repeat the well-worn phrase: "Plan the work and work the plan."

• The development officer is also a *technician*—acting as administrator of the development or campaign office and controller of its systems.

The solid professional, for example, will ensure that all names are spelled correctly—because experience has taught that in fund raising, small details and grand design must come together.

Before you can build or expand a development office, however, the nagging question of *cost* presents itself. There's a good deal of truth in the old bromide,

"You've got to spend money to raise money." The costs of a development operation can be an *investment,* rather than an expense item. If you plan well, the returns will tend to be proportionate to the "front-end" investment.

"It is unwise to pay too much, but worse to pay too little," said John Ruskin. "When you pay too little, you sometimes lose all, because the thing you bought was incapable of doing the thing it was bought to do.

"The common law of business balance prohibits paying little and getting a lot," Ruskin warned. "It can't be done."

In a sense, the development function is like any business operation. The greatest risk for either enterprise is in the early years, when they are most vulnerable to the effects of undercapitalization.

Money, however, is not the only way to attract talented people. They want to work for an organization that has the potential for achievement. It's true that for most professionals, one symbol of the organization's commitment is the front-end investment in the program. Another is its willingness to provide the *time* to build a strong program.

It's not uncommon, for example, for a new annual giving program to "lose money" for a couple of years. In planned giving, it may take longer to bring a commitment to a close. Even more time may be required to get the organization ready to launch a successful capital campaign.

This, of course, is just another way of pointing up the value of "up-front" investment. If time is *not* provided, the development process will degenerate into a series of "shakedowns"—in which the easy money is taken, and the building of relationships neglected.

There are, unfortunately, some professionals who will use a "grace period" to lose themselves in the process—never to be seen again. These nomads move to another organization after a year or two, repeating their act. Fortunately, they are few in number.

In sum, the best development professional is an effective planner, strategist, director, facilitator, communicator and administrator.

Some would say that these terms describe any competent manager in today's business world. That's probably true; for this job description has been modeled for us, to a great extent, by the development officers who *are* in business—the outside fund-raising consultants who are discussed on the following pages.

Counsel Can Help
to Ensure Success

Once an organization has "gone public" with its plans for development, the community's leadership will be watching closely to see what happens. For them, success in fund-raising reflects a well-run outfit.

On the other hand, a program that flounders and falls short of its goal can be a terrible setback to the reputation of any organization. Contributions and volunteers will be harder to come by the next time—which may be a long way off.

Because the outcome is so crucial, many organizations take out an "insurance policy" by engaging professional fund-raising counsel.

The best firms are known for making the goal. After all, *their* reputations—and their survival as businesses—depend on it. They may even be able to "create" a campaign where one didn't seem possible.

Fund-raising consultants are available in various specialties: direct mail, planned giving and the like. This discussion focuses on those which consult on campaigns and ongoing development programs.

These consultants seem to fall into two categories. Some provide part-time services and act primarily as advisors. Others provide on-site direction of a program, usually on a full-time basis.

The consultant who acts only as an advisor may provide service at a lower total cost. He or she may even offer a more advanced approach. A consultant, however, cannot manage volunteers and staff as well as an on-site director.

The solution? Today, many firms provide part-time consultation before the campaign; then full-time, resident direction during the intensive period. Finally, part-time consultation is made available after the campaign.

In this scenario, the part-time service is usually provided by an officer of the firm, who then supervises the campaign director.

What are the advantages of retaining counsel? Here are the major ones:

First is *independence*. Counsel's autonomy can make it easier for them to say what needs to be said, and to insist on doing things right. That's because they're not part of the organization's "office politics."

Counsel is also in a position to learn things that might not be shared so candidly with someone closer to the institution. At the same time, because counsel has gained objectivity through many different experiences, it can be easier for them to interpret and analyze many situations—and to recommend the best course of action.

For these reasons, many veteran fund-raisers believe that outside counsel is just about the only agency that can conduct an effective feasibility study.

Another advantage is that counsel can provide the sheer *manpower* (or, today, womanpower) to do the full-time job of directing a campaign—and do it without diversion. Counsel's ability to provide a concentrated effort also lends a sense of urgency to the enterprise.

Counsel can be valuable for any number of other reasons. For example, because they've done it before, they can estimate with a measure of accuracy how much a given program will cost, and how long it will take.

Fund-raising counseling firms charge for their services on a fee basis, in the same way as legal and accounting firms. Most respectable firms will charge a fixed fee, whether the effort exceeds its goal or falls short.

———————

Much of what can be said for the better firms can also be said for the experienced in-house professional. The fund-raising expert, whether on the institution's staff or with a consulting firm, knows what *must* be done and what is superfluous.

Beware of the consultant (or the staffer) who agrees with you on everything. Either they're not being honest or they're duplicating your own efforts. As William Wrigley used to say, "When two people agree all the time, one of them is unnecessary."

Those who have been through the fires of selecting counsel often offer this advice: Beware of the slick sales presentation which provides an easy answer to every difficult question. Instead, look for evidence that the firm has *listened* to you—and wants to design a program for *your* specific situation.

Certainly, it's possible to misuse counsel. Among the most common mistakes in dealing with counsel are:

- Forgetting that the "meter is always running."
- Ignoring advice on a regular basis.
- Failing to disclose important information.

One last advantage of working with counsel: They are part of the business community, and as such, are likely to have a keen sense of the values and concerns of donors. I'll never forget Carlton Ketchum's early edict to his campaign directors: "Always wear a hat and never smoke a cigar."

Quotations

*"Colors fade, temples crumble, empires
fall, but wise words endure."*

—THORNDIKE

These quotations are presented to assist
in our continuing quest to inspire
potential benefactors and advocates.

Philanthropy

These Americans are peculiar people. If, in a local community, a citizen becomes aware of a human need which is not being met, he thereupon discusses the situation with his neighbors. Suddenly, a committee comes into existence. The committee thereupon begins to operate on behalf of the need and a new community function is established. It is like watching a miracle, because these citizens perform this act without a single reference to any bureaucracy, or any official agency.

—ALEXIS DE TOQUEVILLE

Apart from the ballot box, philanthropy presents the one opportunity the individual has to express his meaningful choice over the direction in which our society will progress.

—GEORGE G. KIRSTEIN

We make a living by what we get, but we make a life by what we give.

—Winston Churchill

―――

The highest use of capital is not to make more money, but to make money do more for the betterment of life.

—Henry Ford

―――

America is a willingness of the heart.

—F. Scott Fitzgerald

―――

If a man is willing to give, the value of his gift is in its proportion to what he has.

—St. Paul's Letter
to the Corinthians

―――

To give away money is an easy matter and in any man's power. But to decide to whom to give it, and how large and when, and for what purpose and how, is neither in every man's power—nor an easy matter. Hence it is that such excellence is rare, praiseworthy and noble.

—Aristotle

Voluntarism

Money is not given,
It has to be raised.

Money is not offered,
It has to be asked for,

Money does not come in,
It must be "gone after."

—ANONYMOUS

One thing I know: The only ones among you who will be really happy are those who will have sought and found how to serve.

—ALBERT SCHWEITZER

The impersonal hand of government can never replace the helping hand of a neighbor.

—HUBERT HUMPHREY

It is one of the beautiful compensations of this life that no one can sincerely try to help another without helping himself.

—RALPH WALDO EMERSON

The fruit should pray for the welfare of the leaves.

—YIDDISH SAYING

———

No man is an island, entire of itself; every man is a piece of the continent, a part of the main; . . . any man's death diminishes me, because I am involved in mankind.

—JOHN DONNE

———

The underlying philosophy of corporate philanthropy is that it is good business to be an enlightened corporate citizen. It doesn't make sense to talk about successful corporations in a society whose schools, hospitals, churches, symphonies, or libraries are deteriorating or closing.

—CLIFTON C. GARVIN, JR.

Goals and Accomplishments

Where there is no vision, the people perish.

—BOOK OF PROVERBS, 29:18

―――――

Make no little plans; they have no magic to stir men's blood . . . Make big plans, aim high in hope and work.

—DANIEL H. BURNHAM

―――――

I am glad that the eight-hour day had not been invented when I was a young man. If my life had been made up of eight-hour days I do not believe I could have accomplished a great deal.

—THOMAS A. EDISON

―――――

Nothing great is created suddenly, any more than a bunch of grapes or a fig. If you tell me that you desire a fig, I answer you that there must be time. Let it first blossom, then bear fruit, then ripen.

—EPICTETUS

―――――

The biggest things are always the easiest to do because there is no competition.

—WILLIAM VAN HORNE

For purposes of action nothing is more useful than narrowness of thought combined with energy of will.

—HENRI FREDERIC AMIEL

Out of the strain of the Doing,
Into the peace of the Done.

—JULIA LOUISE WOODRUFF

About the Author

James Gregory Lord has served virtually every type of philanthropic organization through his work as an independent consultant, as well as with two of the largest firms in the fund-raising field. He has been involved in more than one hundred capital and annual campaigns—providing supervision, marketing consultation and on-site campaign direction. *The Raising of Money* draws numerous examples from this experience—including, most recently, a successful $20 million university program.

Mr. Lord's first book, *Philanthropy and Marketing*, is widely recognized as the first and best work on the application of marketing principles to fund raising. It has been called "a classic in the field," and has received worldwide acclaim. It is in its seventh printing in less than three years.

Mr. Lord's career includes experience in both the business and non-profit sectors. He began his career in philanthropy sixteen years ago as a staff member of the United Way in Cleveland, Ohio—one of the nation's leading United Way organizations. Before becoming an officer of a national consulting firm, he pursued a career in public relations and journalism, serving as an editor in radio, television and newspapers.

Mr. Lord's articles have appeared in most of the leading journals in the fund-raising field. For the National Society of Fund Raising Executives, he helped to develop the examination now being used in the certification of fund-raising executives. He serves on the faculty of the NSFRE Institute.

In the past year, more than 2,000 people have attended Mr. Lord's speeches and seminars. He is currently writing a new work on marketing communications.

About the Editor

Derek VanPelt is Director of Special Projects for Goettler Associates, Inc., a national fund-raising counseling firm based in Columbus, Ohio. He is responsible for the development of campaign marketing programs for the firm's clients, and also for the firm's own marketing communications.

Before entering the fund-raising field, Mr. VanPelt worked for ten years as a writer, editor, designer and public relations consultant. He was involved in the development of several successful publishing ventures—including a national newsletter, two city magazines and a regional arts and entertainment magazine.

Mr. VanPelt also edited James Gregory Lord's first book, *Philanthropy and Marketing*.

Suggested Reading

Fund Raising

Ardman, Perri and Harvey, *The Woman's Day Book of Fund Raising*. New York, St. Martin's, 1980.

Brakeley, George A., Jr., *Tested Ways to Successful Fund Raising*. New York, American Management Association, 1980.

Broce, Thomas E., *Fund Raising: The Guide to Raising Money from Private Sources*. Norman, University of Oklahoma Press, 1979.

Gurin, Maurice G., *What Volunteers Should Know for Successful Fund Raising*. Briarcliff Manor, Stein & Day, 1980.

National Catholic Development Conference, *Bibliography of Fund Raising & Philanthropy*. Washington D.C., National Catholic Development Conference, 1982.

O'Connell, Brian, Ed., *America's Voluntary Spirit: A Book of Readings*. New York, The Foundation Center, 1983.

Seymour, Harold J., *Designs for Fund-Raising: Principles, Patterns, Techniques*. New York, McGraw, 1966.

Sharpe, Robert F., *Before You Give Another Dime*. Nashville, Thomas Nelson Publishers, 1979.

Numerous titles are also available from the Public Management Institute, San Francisco; Taft Corporation, Washington, D.C.; The Foundation Center, New York; and The Grantsmanship Center, Los Angeles.

Marketing

Perhaps the best-known scholar and author on the application of marketing principles to non-profit organizations is Philip Kotler. His current work is *Marketing for Non-Profit Organizations (Revised Edition)*.

Periodicals

CASE Currents, Council for the Advancement and Support of Education, 11 Dupont Circle, Washington, D.C. 20036.

Foundation News, The Foundation Center, 1828 L Street, N.W., Washington, D.C. 20036.

FRI Monthly Portfolio, Fund-Raising Institute, Box 365, Ambler, Pennsylvania 19002.

Fund Raising Management, 224 Seventh Street, Garden City, New York 11530.

NSFRE Journal, National Society of Fund-Raising Executives, Investment Building, 1511 K Street, N.W., Washington, D.C. 20005.

501(c)(3)Monthly Letter, P.O. Box 6401, Evanston, IL 60204   906/884-2397

Films

To Care: America's Voluntary Spirit. Produced by Independent Sector, Washington, D.C. Available from Films Incorporated, 633 Green Bay Road, Willamette, Illinois 60091. Telephone (toll free): (800) 323-4222.

Index

Administrator, 102
Advocate, i, 21, 95, 97; *also see* investment counsellor
American Association of Fund-Raising Counsel, vi
Amiel, Henri Frederick, 116
Annual programs, 57
Aristotle, 112
Asking, 87; *also see* solicitation
Attitudes, 12; *also see* interests
Awareness program, 15, 36, 37; *also see* cultivation

Belzberg, Samuel, 27
Berra, Yogi, 32
Bible, 88, 115
Black and Decker, 8
Boys Clubs of America, 5
Budget, 35, 102
Burnham, Daniel, H., 115

Campaign cabinet, 53
Campaign executive committee, *see* campaign cabinet
Campaign headquarters, 27
Capital campaign, 9, 10, 12, 13, 16, 20, 21, 32, 67, 103
Carroll, Lewis, 66
Case for support, 18, 19, 20, 40
Cervantes, 49
Charity, 4, 5
Churchill, Winston, x, 112
Climate, 39, 62, 68
Colleges; universities, 4, 8, 9, 10, 16, 19, 20, 21, 28, 29, 30, 51, 56, 84
Commemorative opportunities, 57, 87
Community asset, 6
Competition, 7, 8
Confidentiality, 40
Consultant, 39, 40, 76, 104, 105, 106, 107, 108
Corporations, 75, 84
Cost, 102
Counsel, *see* consultant
Coward, Noel, 86
Cultivation, 15, 36, 37, 38, 42

Dahlkemper, Joseph B., v
Deadlines, 61, 62, 67, 71
Deficit, 6
Demographics, 34
Designs for Fund Raising, vi
Distinctive competency, 9
Donne, John, 114
Donor community, 12, 14
Drucker, Peter, 77

Edison, Thomas A., 115

Emerson, Ralph Waldo, 113
Epictetus, 115
Evaluations, *see* prospect evaluations
Exchange, 5

Feasibility study, 16, 30, 36, 39, 40, 42, 106
Fees, 107
Fitzgerald, F. Scott, 112
Ford, Henry, 63, 112
Franklin, Benjamin, 14, 50
Freyd, William, 66
Foundations, 75
Fuller, Buckminster, 65

Garvin, Clifton C., Jr., 114
Giving clubs, 57
General chairman, 30
Goettler Associates, Inc., 63

Hard sell, 77
Hospitals, 8, 16, 27, 33, 36, 37, 41, 42, 84; *also see* medical center
Humphrey, Hubert, 113
Hurok, Sol, 68
Huxley, Aldous, 42

Insistent voice, 102
Institutional Development Counsel, 66
Interests, 6, 8, 10, 12, 16, 21; *also see* attitudes
Interpersonal skills, 101
Interviews, 15, 16
Investment; investor, 4, 5, 7, 10, 18, 19, 20, 37, 41, 99
Investment counsellor, 73, 86
Involvement, 31, 40, 42

Job description, 62
Jones, James A., 63, 64

Kelly, George, 15
Ketchum, Carlton, 108
Ketchum, Inc., vi, 70
Kirstein, George G., 111

Leadership awareness program, *see* awareness program, cultivation program
Ledru-Rollin, Alexandre, 11
Leighton, Dr. Dorothea, 17
Lincoln, Abraham, 13, 68

Management, 101, 104
Marketing, 1, 7, 19, 32, 39, 72
Medical center, *see* hospitals
Metropolitan Opera, 9
Meetings, 70
Milestones, 64, 67; *also see* deadline

126

Mission, 34, 35
Motivations, 16
Museums, 8, 55
Napoleon, 4
National 4-H Council, 91
National Society of Fund Raising
    Executives, 120
Needs, 3, 6, 14, 18

Oates, James F., 52
Official family, 54
Opera, 9

Pace-setting, 40, 64
Pascal, ix
Pasteur, Louis, 86
Pathway, access, 85
People's Republic of China, 9
Performing arts groups, 8
Persuasion, 76
Plan; planning, 19, 32, 34, 36, 37,
    38, 42, 63
Plan, business, 33
Plan, financial, 33
Plan, fund-raising, 35, 37
Planned giving, 58, 103
Pledge period, see subscription
    period
Pogo, 63
Policy, 31
Positioning, 7, 8, 9, 10
Preferences, 12; also see interests
Princeton University, 52
Priorities, see interests
Project management, 61
Prospect evaluation, 83, 84, 85
Prospect research, 84
Public relations, 38
Public television and radio, 11

Quid pro quo, 31

Raise the sights, 57
Ratner, Albert, 87
Reagan, President, 20
Recruiting, 81, 101
Red China, 9
Research, see project research
Responsive chord, 21
Revlon, 8
Revson, Charles, 8
Ries, Al, 9
Rockefeller, John D., 4, 76, 81
Rogers, Will, 88
Ruskin, John, 103
Rule of thirds, 48
Ruth, Babe, 87

Schedule; scheduling, 35, 62, 63, 65,
    66, 102; also see deadlines,
    milestones
Schreyer, R. Blair, vi, 70
Schweitzer, Albert, 113
Self-image, 17
Selling, 8
Seneca, 32, 91
Sequence, 64
Services, 34, 35
Seymour, Harold, J., vi, 17, 25, 49
Shakespeare, William, viii
Slogan, 9, 21
Social service organizations, 8
Socrates, 80
Solicitation, 40, 80, 87, 101;
    also see asking
St. Paul, 112
Stance, 7, 10
Standards chart, 41, 47, 48, 83
Steiner, George, A., 32
Strategic Planning, 32, 34
Strategic plans, 33, 34, 42
Strategists, 79, 102
Studies, see surveys, feasibility
    studies
Subscription period, 56
Surveys, 33, 40
Surveys, mail, 15
Surveys, telephone, 15
Snyergy, 65

Table of investments, see
    standards chart
Tactics, 40
Talmud, 78
Tax benefits, 56, 57
Technician, 102
Test market, 38
Theatres, 6
Theme, 9
Third Sector, iii
Thorndike, 109
Timetable, see schedule
Tolstoy, 46
Top ten, 47
Toqueville, Alexis de, 111
Training, 102
Trout, Jack, 9
Trustees, 52, 56

United Way, 119
Universality, 68; also see climate
University, see colleges

Values, see interests
Van Horne, William, 115

VanPelt, Derek, vi
Vision, 18, 19

Wants, *see* needs
War and Peace, 46
Wilde, Oscar, 67
Woodruff, Julia Louise, 116
Wrigley, William, 107

YMCA, 93

Zoos, 13

Notes

Notes

Notes

Notes

Notes

Notes

Notes

Notes

Notes

Notes